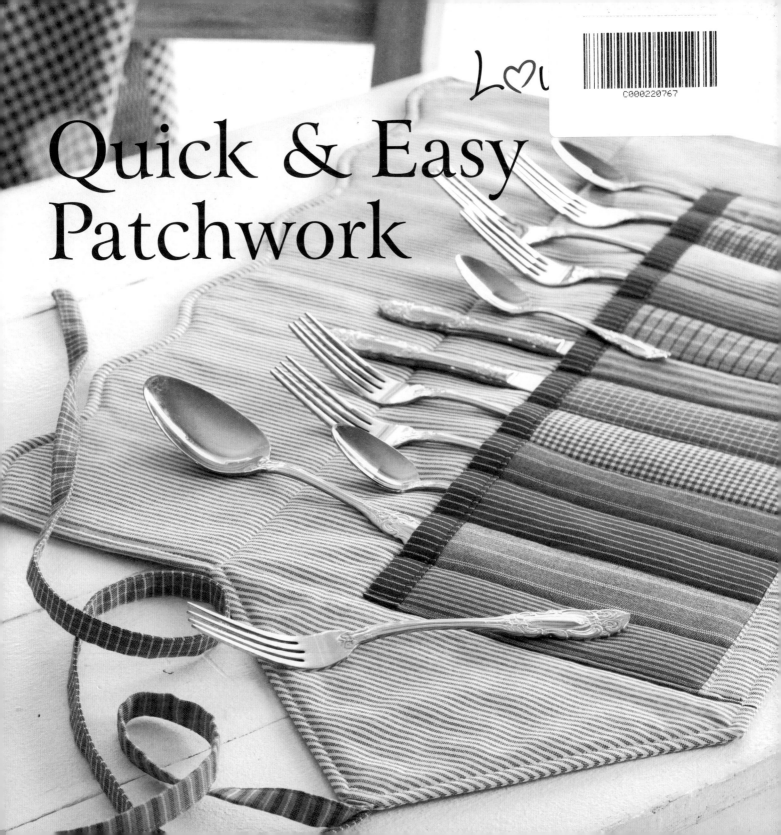

Quick & Easy
Patchwork

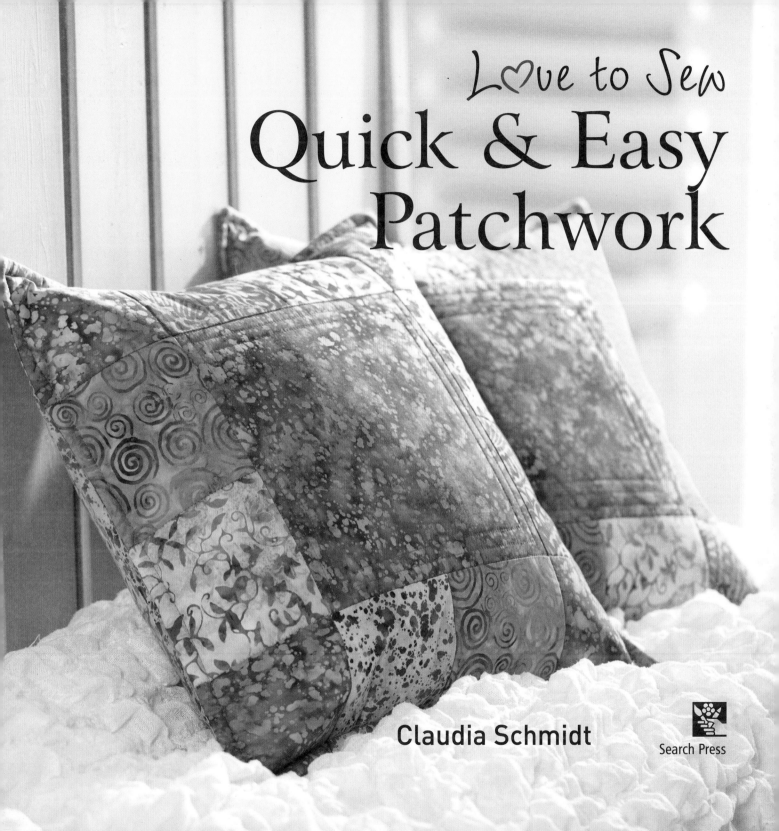

Love to Sew

Quick & Easy
Patchwork

Claudia Schmidt

Search Press

First published in Great Britain 2016 by Search Press Limited
Wellwood, North Farm Road, Tunbridge Wells, Kent TN2 3DR

Original German edition published as *Patch easy!*

Copyright © 2014 Christophorus Verlag GmbH,
Freiburg/Germany

Text copyright © Claudia Schmidt 2014

English translation by Burravoe Translation Services

ISBN: 978-1-78221-299-7

Designs: Claudia Schmidt
Technical drawings: Claudia Schmidt
Photography: Uli Glasemann
Styling: Elke Reith

Printed in China

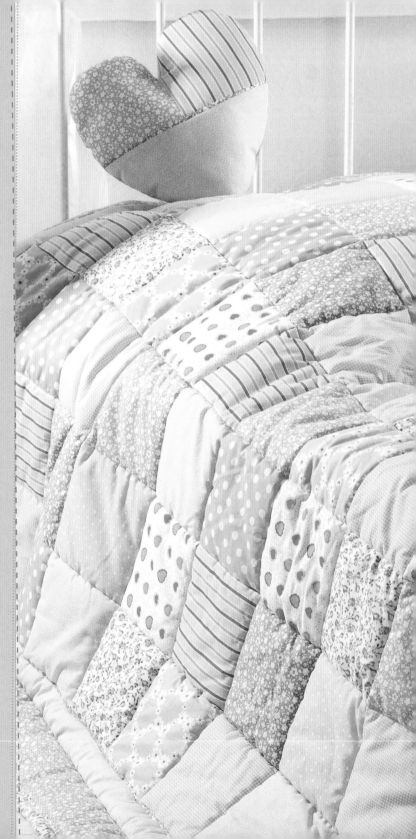

Contents

Shopping Bag, page 14

Rainbow Pillow, page 18

Cutlery Roll, page 22

Patchwork Bedroom, page 26

Scrapbook Covers, page 32

Pillow Cover, page 38

Coffee Cosies, page 42

Device Covers, page 46

Make-Up Bag, page 52

Wall Tidy, page 56

Introduction

Small shapes can have a huge impact! Squares, rectangles and stripes can be combined with ease to create the most interesting and charming patterns. You don't need to have professional sewing skills or carry out complicated calculations in order to sew pieces of fabric together and insert zips for your quilt or bag.

The various stages are all explained with step-by-step photographs and the basic instructions, which also include pictures, explain the main sewing steps. You'll find it really easy to copy these ideas or adapt them for your own projects.

There are also lots of little details that add special touches to the projects, such as a little bow, piping in a contrasting colour, a patch pocket or a quirky or unusual shape. By skillfully joining stripes together and using special cuts, you can create patterns that might look complicated – but aren't!

'Easy' is the watchword here. The techniques shown in this book can also be used to create your own designs or make one in the size of your choice: simply lovely – lovely and simple!

With that in mind, I hope you will enjoy spend many happy hours getting creative with your patchwork.

[signature]

The projects are graded according to how easy they are:

Quick and easy ♡
Requires a little practice ♡ ♡
More challenging ♡ ♡ ♡

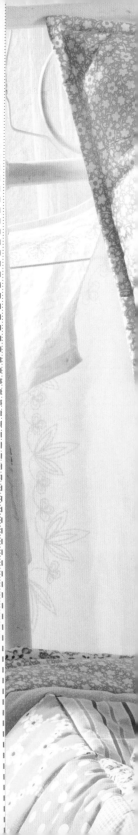

Sewing basics

Ironing

Iron your fabrics before you start to sew and after completing a stage in your work. Be extra careful with synthetic or delicate fabrics; cover them with a clean cotton cloth first to be on the safe side.

Tension

Adjust the tension on your sewing machine to suit the particular fabric; otherwise you could end up with loops in the upper or lower thread. Ideally, always try it out on a test piece first.

Straight stitch

This is the basic utility stitch on a sewing machine. Sewing in straight stitches is also called 'top stitching' if the stitch is visible on the right side of the fabric. You can adjust the stitch length to suit your purposes. The longer the stitch is, the looser the seam will be.

Tacking/basting and pinning

Before sewing, secure the pieces of fabric by tacking/basting a seam by hand or pinning them. This will prevent the pieces of fabric from sliding and creases from forming when you sew them together.

The run of the thread

Every fabric is made up of warp threads (lengthways) and weft threads (crossways). The run of the thread corresponds to the direction of the warp threads, and goes parallel to the selvedge. Always cut fabric in the direction of the run to prevent the fabric from distorting. However, fabric strips that are going to be used to trim rounded fabric edges should be cut at 45° to the selvedge. Trim any selvedge from the fabric before cutting out, as it is never used.

Seam allowance

If a fabric is sewn too close to the edge, the fabric and the seam may easily tear. This is why a seam allowance is added when cutting out. For patchwork and the designs shown in this book, it is 0.75cm (1/3 in).

Right and wrong sides of the fabric

Every piece of fabric has a right and a wrong side. The right side is the side that we see, i.e. the outside of the fabric. This is easy to identify on printed fabrics, as it is the side where the pattern is clearer. So when the instructions tell you to 'place the pieces of fabric with the right sides facing', this means that the right sides (the sides that we normally see) should be together on the inside, and the wrong sides (that we don't normally see) are on the outside. And if the instructions say 'wrong sides facing', then the right sides should be on the outside, and the wrong sides on the inside.

Patterns, templates

The measurements given under 'Cutting out' already include the 0.75cm (1/3in) seam allowance. The pattern pieces tell you whether a seam allowance is included or not.

Fabric fold

Folding a piece of fabric in half creates a folded edge that is called the fold of the fabric or fold line. On a cut piece of fabric, the fold is usually the middle of the item. In this book, the fold is shown as a broken line. This edge of the cut fabric is then placed exactly on the fabric fold without a seam allowance for cutting out.

Zigzag stitch

The zigzag stitch is a very useful utility stitch on a sewing machine. It is mostly used to neaten cut edges. The stitch width and length can be adjusted.

Cutting out

Transfer the template carefully to tracing paper or thin cardboard and cut out a pattern piece. Pin this pattern piece to the wrong side of the fabric and draw around it in tailor's chalk or with a marking pen. Then add any seam allowances on all sides and draw in. Cut out with fabric scissors. Some pattern pieces already include the seam allowance (see instructions).

Note that the small letters (a, b, c etc.) used in the 'Cutting out' sections refer to the different sizes of the pieces. The capital letters (A, B, C, etc.) used in the 'Materials' lists refer to the types of material from which these different-sized pieces are cut.

Materials

It is expected that you will have the following basic items, so they are not listed separately in the instructions.

- ♥ Sewing machine
- ♥ Sewing thread
- ♥ Sewing needles
- ♥ Pins
- ♥ Small sewing scissors
- ♥ Pattern paper, pencil/pen
- ♥ Tailor's chalk
- ♥ Fabric (dressmaking) scissors
- ♥ Cutting knife
- ♥ Seam cutter
- ♥ Tape measure
- ♥ Iron
- ♥ Cutting mat
- ♥ Patchwork ruler
- ♥ Rotary cutter

Sewing techniques

Right sides facing

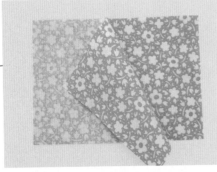

The outside of a fabric is known as the 'right side', so it follows that the inside is known as the 'wrong side'. If two pieces of fabric are to be sewn together, they are placed together with the right sides facing. After sewing them, the seam allowances will be on the back.

Foot width

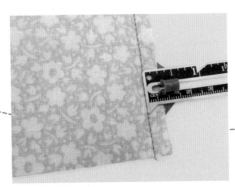

In patchwork, unless stated otherwise, fabrics are sewn together with a seam allowance of 0.75cm (⅓in). This is also known as a 'foot width' because the right edge of the fabric runs parallel to the right edge of the sewing machine foot when sewing.

However, some sewing feet are narrower or wider, so use the needle position to correct the space between the needle and the right edge of the foot.

Seam allowances and seams

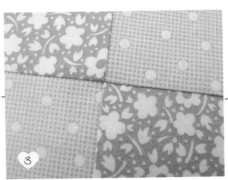

1 In patchwork, always iron all the seam allowances to one side together. If several small units are being sewn together in a row, iron each row's seam allowances in a different direction. Align the vertical seams so they are all flush together before sewing.

2 The seam allowances that are facing in different directions should 'slide' together in the correct positions. Insert a safety pin through the vertical seams and sew the edges together at one foot width.

3 Open out the rows and iron the seam allowances in one direction. The seams will now cross each other perfectly.

Securing seams

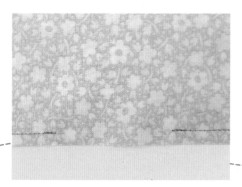

Any seams that are not going to be oversewn again later, for instance at turning openings or visible top stitching seams, are 'secured'. At the beginning of the seam, sew three or four stitches forwards, then three or four stitches back, and then forwards again. Do the same at the end of the seam.

Turning out square shapes

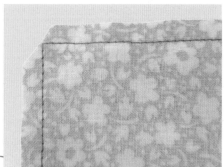

At the corners, trim the seam allowances to just before the seam so the corners are not bulky, and so you can shape the corner neatly after turning the item right side out. If the corners are on the inside, snip a tiny triangle out of the fabric. Careful: Do not use scissors to shape the corners, as they could damage them. Ideally, use a thin piece of wood.

Turning out round shapes

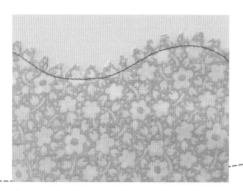

For rounded items, snip tiny triangles into the seam allowances to just outside the seams. This ensures that the corner is nice and flat when the fabric is right side out, as the additional width of the seam allowance is more neatly distributed.

Turning opening

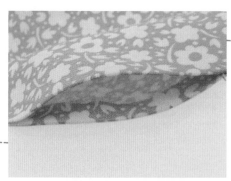

Turn the seam allowances to the inside along the turning openings. Sew up the turning openings by hand using ladder stitch. Insert the needle in the folded edge and draw it through again a little further on, and insert in the opposite folded edge at the same level. Continue like this and tighten the thread after a few stitches. Once you have closed the opening, secure the thread neatly.

Stitching

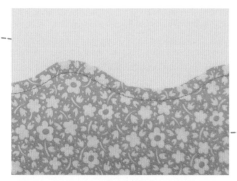

When stitching a seam, make sure you keep an equal distance from the edge. If stitching rounded or curved edges, you can first draw the line with a self-erasing marker pen. 'Edge stitch' means stitching close – about 2–3mm (1/8in) – to the edge.

Making ties

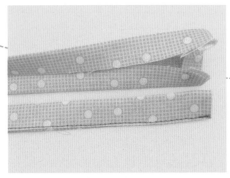

Fold the strip in half lengthways and iron lightly down the fold. Open the strip out again, then fold the two long sides from the outside to the middle fold and iron. Fold the strips in half and iron well. Fold one end over to the inside slightly. Fold the strip again and edge stitch the folded edges neatly.

Inserting ties

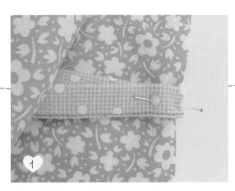

1 Lay the ties on the right side of the fabric with the unfinished ends of the ties at the edge. Place the second piece of fabric on top. Sew along the edge.

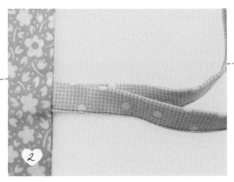

2 When you turn the item right side out, the ties will be on the outside.

Base corners

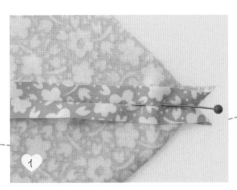

1 The corners are sewn for the base of a bag. Open out the seam allowances and place the side seams or folds on the bottom middle (this could be a seam or a fold).

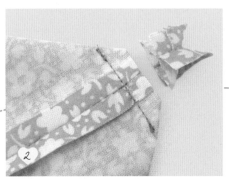

2 Sew across the triangular point in the stated width on both sides, securing the beginning and end well. Trim the triangles back to the width of the seam allowance and neaten.

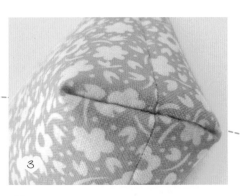

3 Turn the bag through, right side out, to give the corners shape.

Joining strips

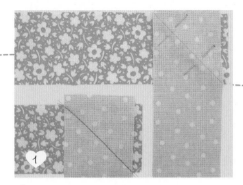
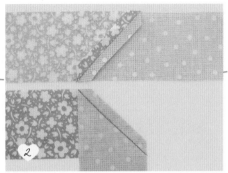
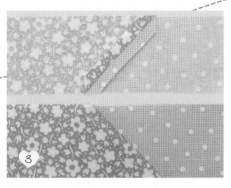

1 Edging for borders is made by joining lots of strips of material together with a diagonal seam (this is a good way of using up fabric remnants). Place the two strips together at a 90° angle with the right sides facing. The ends should protrude slightly. Draw a line at the crossing points and sew the strips together along this line.

2 Trim the protruding fabric back to the width of the seam allowances (as shown in the bottom piece).

The piece on top shows the piece with the fabric trimmed and the seam allowance opened out.

3 Opening the seams allowances and ironing flat will make the seam neater and less conspicuous.

Borders

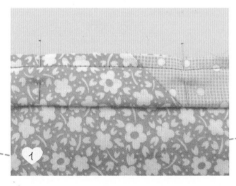
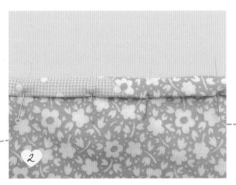
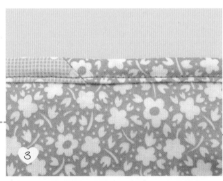

1 To make a border, either fold a strip of fabric four times (see Making ties on page 12), or in half lengthwise with the wrong sides facing.

2 Pin the unfinished fabric edges of the side being edged on the back and edge stitch.

3 Fold the edging over the front covering the seam and edge stitch the front of the folded edge.

Materials

- ♥ A: cotton fabric in natural, 45 x 110cm (17¾ x 43¼in)
- ♥ B: cotton fabric in a light green pattern, 50 x 110cm (19¾ x 43¼in)
- ♥ C–E: 3 different cotton fabrics in light blue/turquoise/green, each 10 x 40cm (4 x 15¾in)
- ♥ F: cotton fabric in light blue, 20 x 110cm (7¾ x 43¼in)
- ♥ G: thin iron-on volume fleece, 45 x 90cm (17¾ x 35½in)

Cutting out

Dimensions including 0.75cm (⅓ in) seam allowance
- ♥ A: 2 rectangles a of 8.5 x 36.5cm (3½ x 14½in) (outside) 2 rectangles b of 22.5 x 36.5cm (9 x 14½in) (outside) 2 strips c of 5.5 x 70cm (2¼ x 27½in) (handles)
- ♥ B: 2 rectangles d of 45 x 36.5cm (17¾ x 14½in) (lining) 4 squares e of 8.5 x 8.5cm (3½ x 3½in) (pattern set)
- ♥ C–E: 4 squares e of 8.5 x 8.5cm (3½ x 3½in) (pattern set)
- ♥ F: 2 strips c of 5.5 x 70cm (2¼ x 27½in) (handles) 4 squares e of 8.5 x 8.5cm (3½ x 3½in) (pattern set)
- ♥ G: 2 strips c of 5.5 x 70cm (2¼ x 27½in) (handles) 2 squares f of 44 x 37cm (17¼ x 14½in) (outsides)

Shopping Bag

Size: 43 x 35cm (17 x 13¾in) without handles • Level of difficulty: ♡

How to do it

1 For the two pattern sets, lay the 20 squares e into four separate rows of five squares and sew the squares together with the right sides facing. Iron the seam allowances for the top and bottom rows of each pattern set in different directions. Sew the top and bottom rows together with the right sides facing, pinning the side vertical seams together so they are lined up perfectly. Open out and iron.

2 For each pattern set, sew one square a to the bottom edge and one rectangle b to the top edge. Iron the seam allowances of the pattern set towards the sewn-on rectangles.

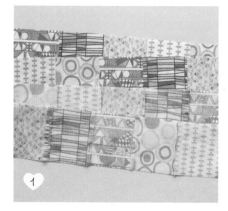
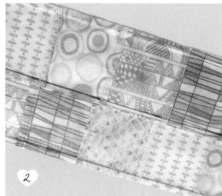

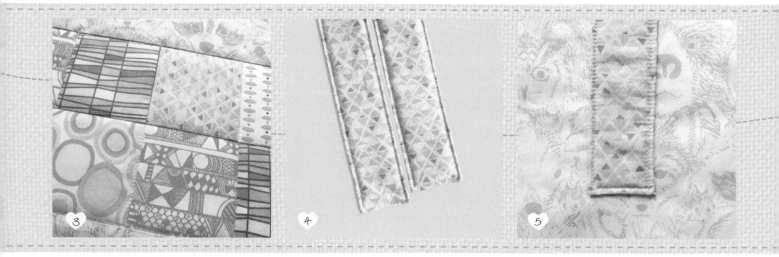

3 Iron the backs of the outsides to fleece G/f and trim the fleece to size. Stitch the squares, sewing the horizontal seams first and then the vertical ones. Seal the beginnings and ends of the vertical seams.

4 For the two handles, iron the strips F/c onto fleece G/c and trim the fleece to size. Place flush on strips A/c with the right sides facing and sew all around, just leaving a turning opening of approx. 15cm (6in) in one long side. Trim the corner seam allowances at an angle and turn the handles right side out. Work the corners and side seams out well and then iron. Sew up the turning openings by hand and attach the handles to fabric F (= outside), working close to the edge.

5 Pin the two ends of a handle to one outside of the bag. The ends should be 14cm (5½in) from the top edge and 9cm (3½in) from the side edges. Sew the ends of the handles to the existing seams on the outside of the bag, stopping 3cm (1¼in) from the top. Sew the handle on diagonally at this point.

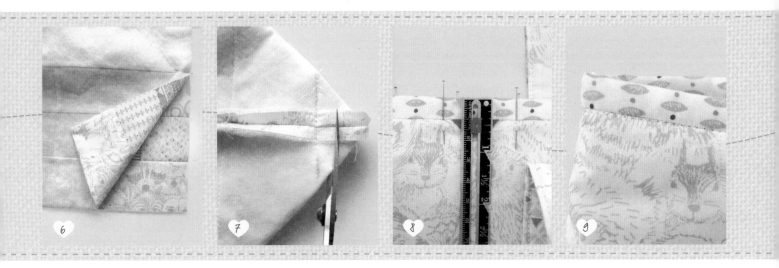

6 Place the outsides together with the right sides facing, making sure the horizontal seams of the pattern piece are lined up, and pin. Sew along the side and bottom edges.

7 For the lining, place the two rectangles together with the right sides facing. Sew along the long sides and one short side, leaving a turning opening of approx. 15cm (6in) on one side edge. For the base corners of the outer piece and lining, align the side seam flush over the base seam, and sew the corner diagonally 3cm (1¼in) from the side/bottom seam. Trim the base corners back to the seam allowance from the seam.

8 Turn the lining right side out and put inside the outer piece. Line up the top edges and side seams and secure. Sew all around the top edges of the outer piece and lining.

Turn the bag right side out and shape the corners well. Fold the seam allowances of the turning opening to the inside and edge stitch along the opening with the machine.

Place the lining against the top edge of the fabric on the inside with the seam on the outside and the lining protruding up on the outside edge by approx. 1cm (½in).

9 Secure the top edge and sink-stitch all round. Increase the stitch length slightly (to 3mm/⅛in). Seal the beginnings and ends of the seams.

Rainbow Pillow

Size: 40 x 80cm (15¾ x 31½in) • Level of difficulty: ♡

Materials

- A–P: 16 different cotton fabrics in rainbow colours, each 10 x 30cm (4 x 11¾in) (12 fabrics only) or 10 x 70cm (4 x 27½in) (6 fabrics only)
- Q: cotton fabric in a black/charcoal pattern, 115 x 110cm (45¼ x 43¼in)
- R: thick iron-on volume fleece, 45 x 85cm (17¾ x 33½in)
- 1 pillow pad, 40 x 80cm (15¾ x 31½in)

Cutting out

Dimensions including 0.75cm (⅓ in) seam allowance
- A–P: 1 each strip a of 6.5 x 30cm (2¾ x 11¾in) (front side) total of 6 different strips b of 6.5 x 40cm (2¾ x 15¾in) (ties for the bows)
- Q: 4 strips c of 6.5 x 110cm (2¾ x 43¼in) (front) 1 rectangle d of 31.5 x 81.5cm (12½ x 32¼in) (back top) 1 rectangle e of 13 x 81.5cm (5 x 32¼in) (back top) 2 rectangles f of 11.5 x 81.5cm (4½ x 32¼in) (back bottom)

How to do it

1 Cut all 16 fabrics A–P into strips 6.5cm (2¾in) wide and arrange in a pretty sequence.

2 Following the diagram, cut the strips A–P/a and Q/c into the lengths indicated. The dimensions include seam allowances. The dimensions for fabric Q also have 2cm (¾in) as a reserve so that the finished front can be trimmed exactly to size later on and any unevenness corrected.

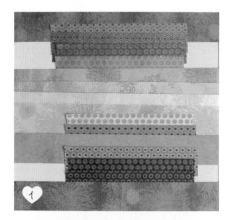

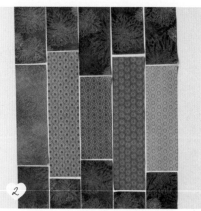

15	A: 21	12,5
12,5	B: 26	10
16,5	C: 17	15
10	D: 27,5	11
14	E: 21,5	13
10,5	F: 29,5	8,5
12,5	G: 25	11
16,5	H: 17	15
11,5	I: 25	12
15	J: 17	16,5
12,5	K: 25,5	10,5
15,5	L: 19,5	13,5
10	M: 28	10,5
13	N: 23	12,5
11	O: 30	7,5
14	P: 19	15,5

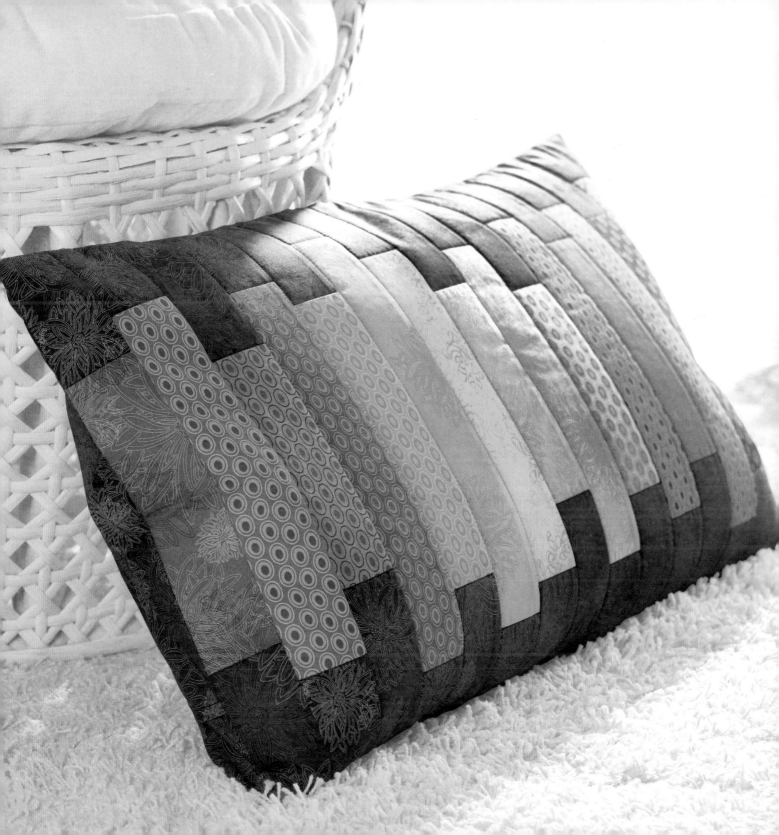

3 First sew the short ends of the rows of two strips of Q and one strip of A–Q together. Iron the seam allowances towards the coloured strip. Sew the rows together to make a larger piece of fabric and iron the seam allowances as you like (but always in the same direction). Iron the back onto fleece R, trimming all round afterwards.

4 Sink-stitch all the strips in matching yarn. Sew strip Q in black and strips A–P differently. Sink-stitch the short crossways seams onto strip Q using black yarn. Secure the beginnings and ends of the seams (except at the top and bottom edges of the pillow front). Now trim the finished front to exactly 41.5 x 81.5cm (16½ x 32¼in), making sure that the seams are parallel or 90° to the side edges.

5 For the ties, fold strips b in half lengthways with the wrong sides facing. Iron, then open out and fold the long sides into the middle. Iron the folds and fold the ties in half lengthways. Sew the folded edges together, working close to the edge, and fold a short edge to the inside by about 0.5cm (¼in) to neaten.

6 For the top half of the back, pin the unfinished ends of three ties to one long right side of rectangle d. The tie with the neatened end will be on the fabric. The outer ties are 20.5cm (8in) from the side edges. Pin the middle tie right to the centre. Pin rectangle e neatly on top with the right sides facing. Sew the edges together with the ties in between.

7 Fold rectangle e to the wrong side of rectangle d. Shape the seam well, then iron and sew the fold line one sewing foot from the edge. Fold the unfinished fabric edge of rectangle e over by one seam allowance twice and edge stitch to rectangle d.

8 For the bottom half of the back, place the two rectangles f together neatly with the right sides facing, and fit the remaining three ties between them as with the other back piece. Open out the rectangles. Iron the seam allowances over to the planned bottom edge. Edge stitch along the right side of the seam to set, making sure you don't accidentally include the ties.

9 Place the top half of the back wrong side to right on the bottom half. The seams with the ties between should be together. Align the ties to each other. Sew the two halves together by approx. 11cm (4¼in) down the sides, sewing onto the existing seam of the top half.

10 Pin the back to the front with the right sides facing, making sure the ties are safe on the inside so they aren't accidentally sewn in. Sew the front and back together on all sides. Trim the corners at an angle. Turn the pillow cover right side out and shape the seams and corners well. Carefully iron the seams on the back so they are flat.

11 Put the pad inside the cover and tie up the bows.

Cutlery Roll ♡♡

Size: 40 x 70cm (15¾ x 27½in) opened without ties • Level of difficulty: ♡ ♡

Materials

- ♥ A: cotton fabric in blue/ecru stripes, 50 x 150cm (19¾ x 59in)
- ♥ B: 12 different cotton fabrics in blue checks/stripes, each 20 x 6cm (7¾ x 2½in)
- ♥ C: cotton fabric in dark blue stripes, 25 x 50cm (9¾ x 19¾in)
- ♥ D: 2 different cotton fabrics in blue checks/stripes, each 5 x 80cm (2 x 31½in)
- ♥ E: thin iron-on volume fleece, 20 x 50cm (7¾ x 19¾in)
- ♥ F: thick iron-on volume fleece, 45 x 70cm (17¾ x 27½in)
- ♥ self-erasing marker pen
- ♥ bias tape shaper, 25mm (1in) (optional)

Cutting out

Dimensions including 0.75cm (⅓in) seam allowance
- ♥ A: 2 rectangles a of 40 x 72cm (15¾ x 28¼in) (main part)
- ♥ B: 12 different rectangles b, each of 20 x 5.5cm (7¾ x 2¼in) (pattern set cutlery insert)
- ♥ C: 1 rectangle c of 23 x 50cm (9 x 19¾in) (lining cutlery insert)
- ♥ D: 2 different strips d, each of 5 x 80cm (2 x 31½in) (ties)

How to do it

1 To make the pattern set for the cutlery insert, sew the long sides of the 12 rectangles b together. Iron all the seam allowances in one direction. Iron fleece E onto the wrong side (trim the overlaps). Straighten the top edge at 90° to the seams, using a ruler and rotary cutter.

2 Place rectangle c flush against the top edge of the cutlery insert with the wrong sides facing and sew the top edges together. Iron the seam allowance over to the lining. Fold the lining and outside together with the wrong sides facing, shifting the seam by 1cm (½in), and secure. Trim the cutlery bag at 17cm (6¾in) (or to suit your own cutlery) and sew the sides and bottom edges together, leaving a turning opening in the bottom.

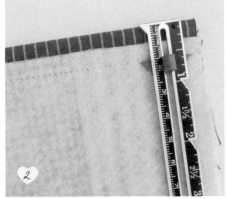

3 Trim the seam allowances at an angle at the corners. Turn the cutlery insert right side out, shaping the corners well, then iron and sew up the turning opening by hand. Edge stitch the lining that is visible on the front on the right side.

4 For the ties, fold strips d in half lengthwise with the wrong sides facing. Iron the folds, then open out and fold one short edge 0.5cm (¼in) to the inside. Place the long sides to the middle and fold the ties over again along the ironed fold. The raw edges will now be on the inside. Alternatively, use a bias tape shaper. Fold a short end of each tape over slightly, then fold the tape in half and edge stitch the folded edges together.

5 For the main section, iron fleece F onto the wrong side of one rectangle a and trim the overlaps (outside). Transfer the sewing lines to the fleece as indicated in the diagram, drawing the wavy edge as per the pattern twice onto the right side edge of the main section at about 1cm (½in) from the top edge (total 60cm/23½in). Draw a vertical line at the end of the wavy edge and draw on the flap. Place both rectangles a together with the right sides facing and secure within the drawn sewing lines. Push the two ties between them and secure the unfinished edges to the tip of the flap (secure the ties safely to the inside so they are not accidentally included).

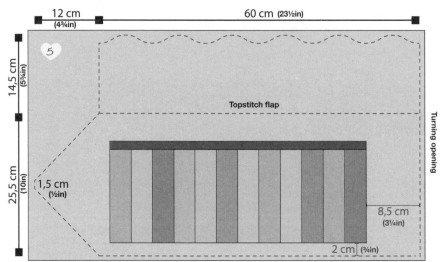

6 Sew all the layers together along the drawn line, leaving a 15cm (6in) turning opening. Be very careful when working along the wavy line and secure at the beginning and end of the seam (at the turning opening). Trim the item 0.75cm (⅓ in) from the seam. Trim the corner seam allowances at an angle and cut tiny triangles out on the inner corner and along the wavy seam until just before the seam. Turn right side out. Shape the corners and wavy edge well, and sew up the turning opening by hand. Sew the item all around the inside about 0.7cm (⅓ in) from the outer edge.

7 To make the wavy seam particularly successful, it's a good idea to draw it first with a self-erasing marker pen. For the flap, draw a line from the end above the flap to the opposite side edge, parallel to the bottom edge (see diagram as well). Pin the inside and outside along the line and sew.

8 Secure the cutlery insert to the lining of the main part. It should be 2cm (¾in) from the bottom edge and 8.5cm (3½in) from the edge of the right side. Sew the sections of the cutlery insert, sewing from top to bottom in sink-stitch and along the top edge of the panel. Finally, sew the side edges and the bottom edge of the insert.

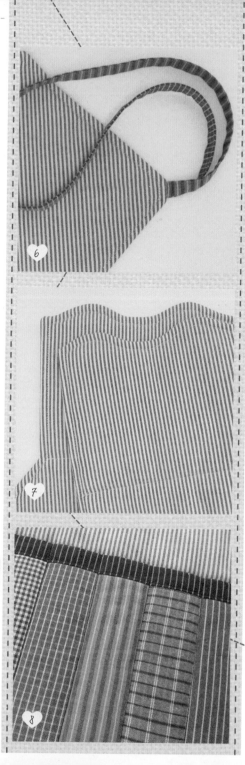

Patchwork Bedroom
Princess Quilt

Size: 224 x 164cm (88 x 64½in) • **Level of difficulty:** ♡ ♡ ♡

Materials

- A: cotton fabric with pink flowers on a light background, 480 x 110cm (189 x 43¼in)
- B: pink floral fabric, each 130 x 110cm (51 x 43¼in)
- C–G: 2 different cotton fabrics in a pink pattern, each 40 x 110cm (15¾ x 43¼in)
- H: cotton fabric in a dark green pattern, 55 x 110cm (21¾ x 43¼in)
- I: cotton fabric in a pale green pattern, 85 x 110cm (33½ x 43¼in)
- J: cotton fabric in a fresh green pattern, 40 x 110cm (15¾ x 43¼in)
- K: thick polyester volume fleece, 235 x 175cm (92½ x 69in)
- crepe tape, safety pins
- sewing machine with top feed, zip foot
- self-erasing marker pen

Cutting out

Dimensions including 0.75cm (⅓ in) seam allowance

- A–G: 12 squares a of 16.5 x 16.5cm (6½ x 6½in) (front middle)
- H–J: 11 squares a of 16.5 x 16.5 cm (6½ x 6½in) (front middle)
- A: 2 rectangles h of 185 x 110cm (73 x 43¼in) (back) 1 rectangle i of 28 x 110cm (11 x 43¼in) (back) 1 rectangle j of 28 x 76.5cm (11 x 30¼in) (back)
- B: join together 7 strips of 11.5 x 110cm (4½ x 43¼in) to approx. 770cm (303in) in length, then cut as follows: 2 strips f of 11.5 x 205.5cm (4½ x 81in) (second edge right/left) 2 strips g of 11.5 x 165.5cm (4½ x 65in) (second edge top/bottom)
- H: join together 7 strips of 2 x 110cm (¾ x 43¼in) to approx. 770cm (303in) in length, then cut as follows: 2 strips b of 2 x 196.5cm (¾ x 77½in) (piping right/left) 2 strips c of 2 x 136.5cm (¾ x 53¾in) (piping top/bottom)
- I: join together 7 strips of 6 x 110cm (2½ x 43¼in) to approx. 770cm (303in) in length, then cut as follows: 2 strips d of 6 x 196.5cm (2½ x 77½in) (first edge right/left) 2 strips e of 6 x 145.5cm (2½ x 57¼in) (first edge top/bottom)

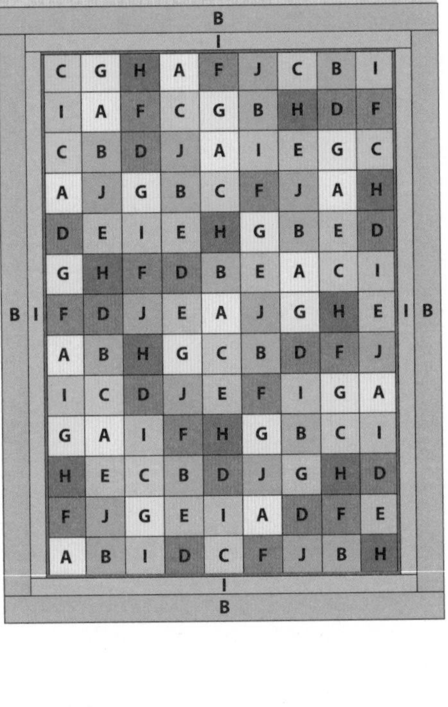

How to do it

1 For the central panel of the front, arrange the squares as shown in the diagram (the capital letters indicate the fabrics). Sew rows of nine squares together to make 13 rows, making sure that if the fabrics have any patterns they are placed correctly.

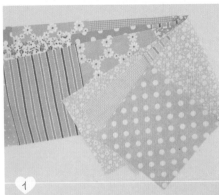

			B					
			I					
C	G	H	A	F	J	C	B	I
I	A	F	C	G	B	H	D	F
C	B	D	J	A	I	E	G	C
A	J	G	B	C	F	J	A	H
D	E	I	E	H	G	B	E	D
G	H	F	D	B	E	A	C	I
F	D	J	E	A	J	G	H	E
A	B	H	G	C	B	D	F	J
I	C	D	J	E	F	I	G	A
G	A	I	F	H	G	B	C	I
H	E	C	B	D	J	G	H	D
F	J	G	E	I	A	D	F	E
A	B	I	D	C	F	J	B	H

B I (left) ... B (right) · I / B (bottom)

2 Iron the seam allowances in alternate directions in each row. Sew the rows together, positioning the overlapping seams together precisely.

3 For the piping, fold strips b and c in half lengthways with the wrong sides facing, and iron. For the first edge, sew strips d together right and left, catching one piping strip b between each. Iron the seam allowances to the outside.

4 Sew strips e to the top and bottom edges, catching one piping strip c between each. Fold the ends of the piping over to the wrong side by one seam allowance. Insert the piping back in the folded edge and pin between the edge strips d. Iron the seam allowances to the outside.

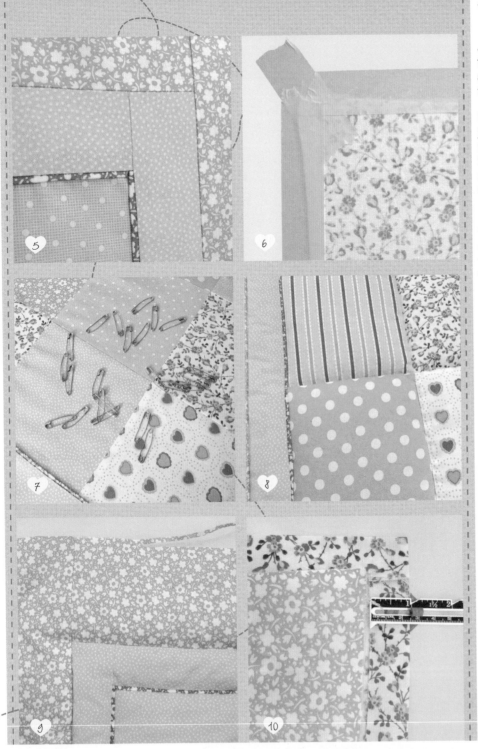

5 For the second edge, sew strips f to the left and right, and strips g to the top and bottom. Iron all the seam allowances to the outside.

6 For the back, first sew rectangles i and j to the short sides, then each rectangle h to a long side. Use crepe tape to attach the back to a large area with the wrong side facing up, making sure it is smooth with no wrinkles.

7 Put the fleece on top, then the front with the right side facing up, and make sure everything is smooth. Secure all the layers together with lots of safety pins. Remove the crepe tape.

8 Increase the stitch length to 3–3.5mm ($1/_8$in) and sew all the seams together between the sink-stitches in matching yarn. Secure the beginnings and ends of the seams. Then sew the middle piece below the piping; use the zip foot, and brush the piping to the side. Finally, sew the seam all round between the first and second edge strips.

9 Remove all the safety pins. Trim the front and fleece until the second edge is only 10cm (4in) wide. Fold the back over so it doesn't get damaged.

10 Trim the back evenly all round so it is 5cm (2in) bigger than the fleece and front. Fold 2.5cm (1in) to the wrong side (inside) and iron.

11 Fold each corner over in half with the right sides facing (to the back) so that the outer edges are neatly positioned together. Draw a line at a right angle in place of the turn on the folded edge, and sew (see broken line). Secure the beginnings and ends of the seams. Trim the overlapping triangle to seam allowance width. Open out the seam allowances.

12 Turn the corners and side edges around the fleece and front right side out. Pin and edge stitch the inner folded edge all round using stitch length 3–3.5mm (⅛in).

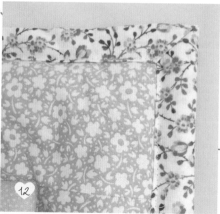

Square Pillow

Size: 80 x 80cm (31½ x 31½in) • **Level of difficulty:** ♡ ♡ ♡

Note

It is useful to have a sewing machine that can sew thick layers and has a top feed so that the layers don't slip when sewing as this can cause folds or creases.

Materials

- A: cotton fabric with pink flowers on a light background, 20 x 20cm (7¾ x 7¾in)
- B: pink floral cotton fabric, 90 x 110cm (35½ x 43¼in)
- C: pink cotton fabric in a delicate pattern, 65 x 85cm (25½ x 33½ inches)
- D: pink cotton fabric with large white dots, 125 x 110cm (49¼ x 43¼in)
- E–F: 2 different cotton fabrics in a pink pattern, each 20 x 40cm (7¾ x 15¾in)
- G: cotton fabric in a pink pattern, 20 x 20cm (7¾ x 7¾in)
- H: cotton fabric in a dark green pattern, 5 x 100cm (2 x 39½in)
- I: cotton fabric in a pale green pattern, 15 x 110cm (6 x 43¼in)
- K: thick polyester volume fleece, 85 x 85cm (33½ x 33½in)
- crepe tape, safety pins
- sewing machine with top feed, zip foot
- 1 pillow pad, 80 x 80cm (31½ x 31½in)

Cutting out

Dimensions including 0.75cm (⅓ in) seam allowance

- ♥ A: 1 square a of 16.5 x 16.5cm (6½ x 6½in)
- ♥ B: 1 square a of 16.5 x 16.5cm (6½ x 6½in)Join together 3 strips of 15 x 110cm (6 x 43¼in) to make a length of approx. 330cm (130in), then cut as follows: 2 strips e of 15 x 55.5cm (6 x 22in) (second edge right/left) 2 strips f of 15 x 82.5cm (6 x 32½in) (second edge top/bottom)
- ♥ C: 1 rectangle h of 60 x 81.5cm (23½ x 32in) (flap closure top)
- ♥ D: 2 squares a of 16.5 x 16.5cm (6½ x 6½in)1 square g of 81.5 x 81.5cm (32 x 32in) (back of the front) 1 rectangle i of 35 x 81.5cm (13¾ x 32in) (flap closure bottom)
- ♥ E: 2 squares a of 16.5 x 16.5cm (6½ x 6½in)
- ♥ F: 2 squares a of 16.5 x 16.5cm (6½ x 6½in)
- ♥ G: 1 square a of 16.5 x 16.5cm (6½ x 6½in)
- ♥ H: 4 strips b of 2 x 46.5cm (¾ x 18¼in) (piping)
- ♥ I: join together 2 strips of 6 x 110cm (2½ x 43¼in) to approx. 220cm (86½in) in length, then cut as follows: 2 strips c of 6 x 46.5cm (2½ x 18¼in) (first edge right/left) 2 strips d of 6 x 55.5cm (2½ x 22in) (first edge top/bottom)

How to do it

1 Arrange the squares in three rows of three squares and, as described for the quilt, iron and sew together. For the first edge, sew strips c to the middle piece with piping b in between on the right and left, then strips d to the top and bottom with piping between. For the second edge, sew strips e to the right and left of the edge, and then strips f to the top and bottom of the first edge.

2 Secure the front with fleece and square g with safety pins as described for the quilt, then sink-stitch all the seams. Trim the finished front of the pillow evenly to 81.5 x 81.5cm (32 x 32in). Sew all the layers together all round within the seam allowance using a flat zigzag stitch.

3 For the flap closure, fold rectangles h and i 1cm (½in) over to the wrong side on one long side, then stitch and iron. Push the rectangles with the sewn edges and the right sides up together until they are the same size as the front; rectangle i will be under h. Sew the overlap together on both side edges to about 11cm (4¼in), sewing over the existing seam of rectangle h.

4 With the right sides facing, pin the flap closure flush to the front of the pillow and trim the corners at an angle. Turn the pillow cover right side out. Shape the corners and seams well, and sew all around at 1.5cm (½in) from the edge. This will neaten the seam allowances on the inside.

Materials

- B: pink floral cotton fabric, 20 x 20cm (7¾ x 7¾in)
- F: cotton fabric in pink stripes, 20 x 20cm (7¾ x 7¾in)
- D: pink cotton fabric with large white dots, 35 x 40cm (13¾ x 15¾in)
- H: cotton fabric in a darker green pattern (piping), 3 x 35cm (1¼ x 13¾in)
- I: cotton fabric in a pale green pattern (front), 20 x 35cm (7¾ x 13¾in)
- L: thick iron-on volume fleece, 35 x 35cm (13¾ x 13¾in)
- synthetic cotton wadding
- self-erasing marker pen
- sewing needles and thread

Cutting out

Dimensions including 0.75cm (⅓ in) seam allowance

- B, F: 1 square a each of 16.5 x 16.5cm (6½ x 6½in)
- D: 2 pieces pattern 2 plus 2cm (¾in) seam allowance (back)
- H: 1 strip b of 2 x 31.5cm (¾ x 12½in) (piping)
- I: 1 rectangle c of 16.5 x 31.5cm (6½ x 12½in)
- L: 1 rectangle d of 31.5 x 31.5cm (12½ x 12½in)

4

Heart-Shaped Pillow

Size: 30 x 30cm (11¾ x 11¾in) • Pattern pieces: 2 on page 63
• Level of difficulty: ♡ ♡ ♡

How to do it

1 Sew the two squares a together for the front. Sew rectangle c with the piping between, as described for the quilt, to the bottom edge. Iron the seam allowance down so the piping is on the squares. Iron the front to fleece L and sew all the seams as described for the quilt.

2 For the back, arrange the cut-out pieces together as indicated in the pattern, and sew together along the middle line, leaving a 10cm (4in) turning opening. Iron open the seam allowances. Draw the sewing lines precisely along the back of the fabric exactly as shown in the pattern.

3 Place the back on the front with the right sides facing. The curves of the heart will be on the squares, and the tip facing the green fabric. Align all the middle seams, then pin and sew the heart all round along the drawn line.

4 Trim the seam allowances all round to 0.75cm (⅓in). Snip into the curves and cut off the tip. Turn right side out. Loosely fill with wadding and sew up the turning opening by hand.

Scrapbook Covers

Materials

- ♥ A: firm cotton fabric, light background, blue pattern, 25 x 75cm (9¾ x 29½in)
- ♥ B–E: 4 different firm cotton fabrics in a blue pattern, each approx. 25 x 30cm (9¾ x 11¾in) (3) and 25 x 45cm (9¾ x 17¾in) (1)
- ♥ F: firm cotton fabric in a dark blue pattern, 25 x 140cm (9¾ x 55in)
- ♥ G: firm cotton fabric in a red-and-blue pattern, 20 x 25cm (7¾ x 9¾in)
- ♥ H: firm cotton fabric in natural, patterned, 40 x 140cm (15¾ x 55in)
- ♥ I: thin iron-on volume fleece, 120 x 90cm wide (47¼ x 35½in)
- ♥ J: scrap of thick volume fleece or wadding
- ♥ elastic in red (or a contrasting colour), 9mm (½in) wide, 40cm (15¾in)
- ♥ sewing needles and thread
- ♥ self-erasing marker pen

Cutting out

Dimensions including 0.75cm (⅓in) seam allowance
- ♥ A: 9 rectangles a of 7.5 x 23cm (3 x 9in) (set of strips outside)
- ♥ B–E: total of 10 rectangles a of 7.5 x 23cm (3 x 9in) (set of strips outside) 1 rectangle b of 20.5 x 17cm (8 x 6¾in) (bag lining) 1 motif of choice cut out of any of the fabrics and the matching piece of fabric (closure)
- ♥ F: 2 strips c of 10 x 120cm (4 x 47¼in) (top and bottom edge outside)
- ♥ G: 1 rectangle d of 14.5 x 17cm (5¾ x 6¾in) (bag outside)
- ♥ H: 1 rectangle e of 38 x 120cm (15 x 47¼in) (lining)
- ♥ I: 2 rectangle e of 38 x 120cm (15 x 47¼in)

Book jacket with pockets

Size: 31 x 31 x 3cm (12¼ x 12¼ x 1¼in) • Level of difficulty: ♡

How to do it

1 For the set of strips on the outside, sew one rectangle B–E/a and one rectangle A/a together alternately along the long sides. Iron the seam allowances in one direction. Trim the set of strips exactly to 20.5cm (8in), aligning the seams at 90° to the top and bottom edges. Sew a strip c to the top and bottom edges respectively. Iron the seam allowances towards strips c.

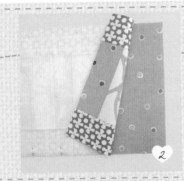   

2 Iron fleece I to the back of the finished outside and lining H. Now trim both pieces exactly to size: the height should be 35cm (13¾in), the width approx. 115.5cm (45½in). Due to the many seams, there may be some slight variation in the individual width, so trim the lining to the width of the outside. Place the outside and front together neatly with the right sides facing and sew together on all sides, leaving a turning opening of about 20cm (7¾in) along the bottom.

3 Trim the corner seam allowances at an angle and turn the item right side out. Shape the corners and seams well. Iron, and secure the layers with a few pins so they don't slip. Sink-stitch all the seams of the set of strips in a matching colour, then sew the side edges, but at a gap of 0.75cm (⅓in) from the top and bottom edges. Then sink-stitch strips c once and then sew again 1cm (½in) from the seam, always 0.75cm (⅓ in) from the side edges.

4 For the pocket, sew the two rectangles b and d together along the 17cm (6¾in) long edge with the right sides facing. Iron the seam allowances towards rectangle b. Fold the item crosswise with the right sides facing and the bottom edges flush together. Sew the side edges and bottom edge together, leaving a turning opening at the bottom, and trim the corner seam allowances at an angle.

5 Turn the pocket right side out. Shape the corners and seams well. Fold the seam allowances along the turning opening to the inside and iron. Sink-stitch the seam between the two fabrics.

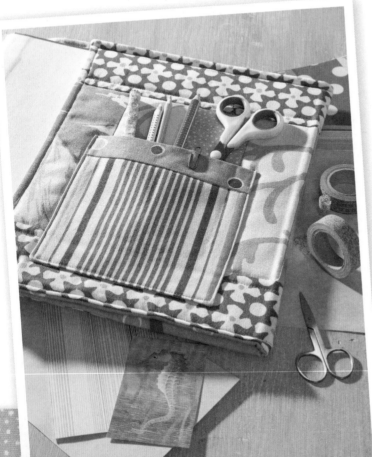

6 For the closure, cut the motif of your choice out of one of the fabrics, and cut out a matching piece of fabric very generously. The motif should be no bigger than 7 x 7cm (2¾ x 2¾in). Draw the planned sewing lines around the motif generously in self-erasing market pen. Cut a scrap of fleece J to the size of the motif.

Place the two cut-out pieces together with the wrong sides facing and secure the fleece between them below the planned outer seams. Include the elastic, positioning it in the middle.

7 Sew around the motif twice, using a slightly shorter stitch length. The seam lines should not match exactly. Trim the fabric all round about 0.7cm (⅓in) from the seam and snip into it a few times to just before the seam. Pluck out any threads of the overlapping fabric with a needle to create a fringed edge.

8 Place the book in the middle of the finished cover and fold the sides evenly over the cover of the book. Close the book. The two main cover pieces should be the same width. Mark the positions with pins. Secure the pocket as desired to the back cover.

9 Take out the book. Open out the cover and edge stitch the pocket to the side and bottom edges. This will also sew up the turning opening.

10 Fold the cover again on both sides as marked. Secure the ends of the elastic in the back of the cover about 8cm (3¼in) from the edge.

11 Tack the folds. Sew along the right side of the top and bottom edges of the book cover, working at a distance of one foot width. This will also secure the cover. Do not sew the elastic, though, but just push it aside. Remove the tacking and put the book inside the cover.

Materials

- A: firm cotton fabric in light blue with polka dots, 25 x 75cm (9¾ x 29½in)
- B: firm cotton fabric in natural with polka dots, 25 x 75cm (9¾ x 29½in)
- C: firm cotton fabric in light blue with a motif, approx. 10 x 60cm (4 x 23½in)
- D: transparent wax cloth or foil, 15 x 25cm (6 x 9¾in)
- white hook and loop fastening, 2cm (¾in) wide, 6cm (2¼in)
- adhesive tape

Cutting out

Dimensions including 0.75cm (¹⁄₃in) seam allowance
- A: 2 rectangles a of 19.5 x 30cm (7¾ x 11¾in) (outside)
- B: 2 rectangles a of 19.5 x 30cm (7¾ x 11¾in) (lining)
- C: 2 motifs of 5 x 9cm (2 x 3½in) plus 2cm seam allowance (¾in) (flap) 2 matching cut-outs for the motifs (flap)
- D: 1 rectangle b of 13 x 22cm (5 x 8¾in) (window)

Scrapbook cover

Size: 18.5 x 30cm (7¼ x 11¾in) • Level of difficulty: ♡

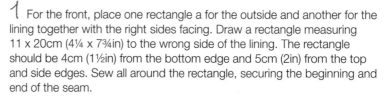

How to do it

1 For the front, place one rectangle a for the outside and another for the lining together with the right sides facing. Draw a rectangle measuring 11 x 20cm (4¼ x 7¾in) to the wrong side of the lining. The rectangle should be 4cm (1½in) from the bottom edge and 5cm (2in) from the top and side edges. Sew all around the rectangle, securing the beginning and end of the seam.

2 Cut a rectangle out of the sewn rectangle 1cm (½in) from the seams. Trim the corners at an angle to just before the seam. Turn the lining and outside right side out. Carefully shape the seams, and iron.

3 For the window, position rectangle b in foil in the middle of the cut-out, secure with a little adhesive tape so it doesn't slide, and sew on the right side in zigzag stitch.

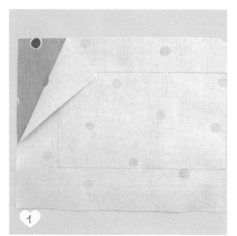

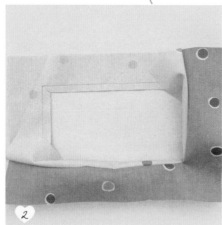

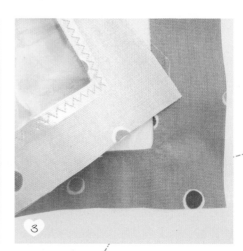

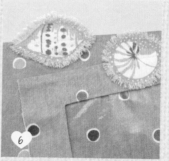

4 Fold the outside and lining to the inside by 0.75cm (in) along the top edge, then iron and sew 1 and 3mm (in) wide. For the back, place the other two rectangles a together with the right sides facing. Sew one long side together (= top edge) and turn over so that the two rectangles now have the wrong sides facing. Carefully iron the top edge and sew like the front. Sew a piece of hook and loop fastening to the middle of the lining at the tops of the front and back.

5 For the two flaps, sew one motif to its counterpart with the wrong sides facing, and sew twice around the motif. The seams should not be exact matches. Cut around the motifs generously. Snip into the seam allowances all around and fringe with a pin. Neaten the fringes somewhat at the end.

6 Sew the flaps to the middles of the top of one front and back piece, sewing the bottom half of the motif and along the top of the flap.

7 Place the insides of the front and back together and sew along the sides and bottom twice, at 1cm (½in) width. The seams should be very slightly offset, or they may cross. Snip into the seam allowances all around to just before the seam at gaps of about 1cm (½in) and fringe with a small pair of sharp scissors or a pin. Neaten the fringes slightly to finish.

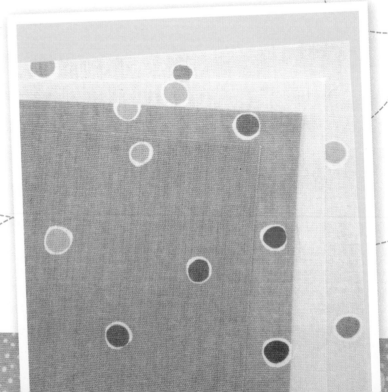

Pillow Cover

Size: each 40 x 40cm (15¾ x 15¾in) • Level of difficulty: ♡

Materials

- A: batik fabric in shocking pink, 25 x 50cm (9¾ x 19¾in)
- B: batik fabric in blue, 50 x 60cm (19¾ x 23½in)
- C–E: 3 different batik fabrics in shades of blue, each 15 x 30cm (6 x 11¾in)
- F: thick iron-on volume fleece, 45 x 45cm (17¾ x 17¾in)
- 1 zip in a colour to match fabric B, 30cm (11¾in)
- 1 pillow pad, 40 x 40cm (15¾ x 15¾in)

Cutting out

Dimensions include 0.75cm (⅓in) or 2cm (¾in) (zip) seam allowance
- A: 1 square a of 21.5 x 21.5cm (8½ x 8½in) (middle square) 4 squares b, each 11.5 x 11.5cm (4½ x 4½in) (edge squares)
- B: 2 squares b of 11.5 x 11.5cm (4½ x 4½in) (edge squares) 1 rectangle c of 12.75 x 41.5cm (5 x 16½in) (back) 1 rectangle d of 32.75 x 41.5cm (13 x 16½in) (back)
- C–E: 2 squares b of 11.5 x 11.5cm (4½ x 4½in) (edge squares)
- F: 1 square e of 41.5 x 41.5cm (16½ x 16½in)

How to do it

1 For the front, arrange squares b around square a (the capital letters in the diagram refer to the fabrics). Sew the four squares of the top and bottom rows together and the two squares at the sides. Iron the seam allowances as desired, and on the rows to the shocking pink corner squares.

2 Sew the side squares (1) to the middle square first, then the top and bottom rows (2). After each step, iron the seam allowances from the middle square to the outside.

3 When sewing the rows together, arrange the seam allowances at the corner squares together. Secure the seams with a pin so they don't slip when sewing.

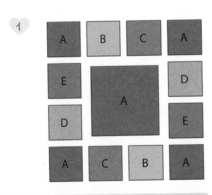

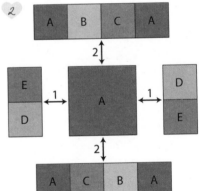

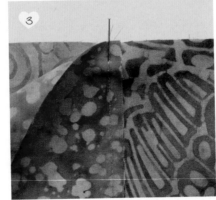

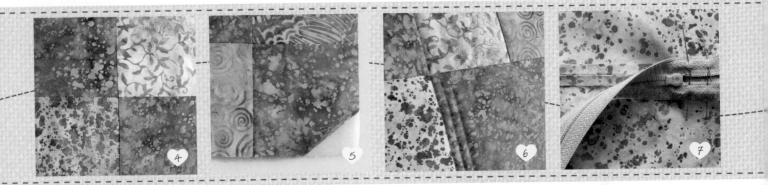

4 The seams should cross exactly.

5 Iron the back of the finished front onto fleece F.

6 Sink-stitch all the seams in matching thread. Sew around the middle square first, then sew the seams between the small squares. Finally, sew twice within the middle square, keeping a foot's distance to the previous seam.

7 For the back, sew the first 5cm (2in) of the long sides of the two rectangles c and d together with 2cm (¾in) seam allowance. Secure the seam. Set a long tacking stitch and return to the normal stitch length 5cm (2in) before the end of the seam. Secure the seam and sew the remaining 5cm (2in). Iron the seam allowances apart and secure the zip to the middle of the tacking, right side to wrong.

8 From the right side, unpick about 10cm (4in) of the tacking on the side with the zip. Fit the zip foot to the sewing machine. Undo the zip a little and sew the zip (right side) along both sides of the entire seam. Make sure you don't get too close to the zip, but lift the foot in time (leaving the needle in the fabric), move the zip, then lower the foot again and continue sewing.

9 Unpick the tacking and remove. Undo the zip.

10 Pin the front and back together neatly with the right sides facing.

11 Sew all around the pieces. Trim the corner seam allowances at an angle and turn the pillow cover right side out. Shape the corners and side seams well, and iron on the back.

Alternative

Work the other pillow in the same way, but instead with only one square a in fabric A, and three (instead of two) squares b in each of the fabrics B–E. Sew the middle square (see step 6) three times instead of twice.

Materials

For 1 small coaster
- ♥ A: cotton fabric in a blackberry red pattern, 5 x 5cm (2 x 2in)
- ♥ B–C: patterned cotton fabric in shades of blackberry, each 5 x 50cm (2 x 19¾in)
- ♥ F: cotton fabric in a blackberry pattern, 15 x 15cm (6 x 6in)
- ♥ G: thin iron-on volume fleece, 15 x 30cm (6 x 11¾in)

Cutting out

Dimensions including 0.75cm (⅓in) seam allowance
- ♥ A: 1 square a of 5.5 x 5.5cm (2¼ x 2¼in) (middle piece)
- ♥ B: 1 strip b of 3.5 x approx. 45cm (1½ x 17¾in) ((first border)
- ♥ C: 1 strip c of 3.5 x approx. 50cm (1½ x 19¾in) (second border)
- ♥ F: 1 square f of 13.5 x 13.5cm (5¼ x 5¼in) (back)
- ♥ G: 2 squares f of 13.5 x 13.5cm (5¼ x 5¼in) (front/back)

Coffee Cosies
Coffee cup mug rug

Size: 12 x 12cm (4¾ x 4¾in) • Level of difficulty: ♡

How to do it

1 For the first border, cut a piece off strip b that is a little longer than the edge of the middle piece, place on an edge of the middle piece with the right sides facing, and sew. Open out the strip. Iron the seam allowances to the outside and trim the edge exactly using a patchwork ruler and rotary cutter.

2 Turn the piece 90° anti-clockwise and cut the next piece off strip b in about the same length as the edge. Sew to the edge as described in step 1. Always iron the seam allowances to the outside. Continue until the middle piece is enclosed (see diagram on page 44).

3 For the second border, sew strip c on as described for the first border until the first border has been completed. Start the second (and every next) border at the same edge as the first border and turn in the same direction (here, anti-clockwise).

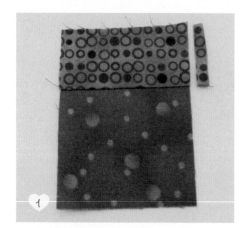

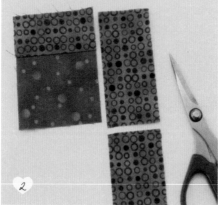

Coffee pot rug

Size: 12 x 12cm (4¾ x 4¾in) • Level of difficulty: ♡

Materials

For 1 large coaster:
- A–C: as for the small coaster
- D: cotton fabric in a blackberry pattern, 5 x 60cm (2 x 23½in)
- F: cotton fabric in a blackberry pattern, 20 x 20cm (7¾ x 7¾in)
- G: thin iron-on volume fleece, 20 x 40cm (7¾ x 15¾in)

Cutting out

Dimensions including 0.75cm (⅓in) seam allowance
- A–C: as for the small coaster
- D: 1 strip d of 3.5 x approx. 60cm (1½ x 23½in) (third border)
- F: 1 square f of 17.5 x 17.5cm (7 x 7in) (back)
- G: 2 squares f of 17.5 x 17.5cm (7 x 7in) (front/back)

4 Iron the fleece onto the wrong sides of the front and back. Place the two pieces together with the right sides facing and sew all around, leaving a turning opening. Trim the corners at an angle. Turn right side out and iron.

5 Sink-stitch the middle piece and the first. Sink-stitch the border in the matching thread.

1. Border for basic block

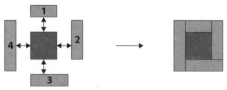

2. Border for coffee cup mug rug

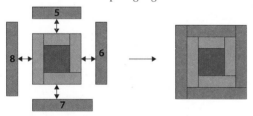

3. Border for coffee pot rug

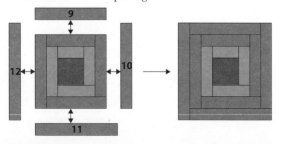

How to do it

Sew and complete as for the small coaster, but add a third border and sink-stitch the second border as well.

Coffee pot cosy

Size: 25 x 20.5cm (9¾ x 8in) • **Level of difficulty:** ♡

Materials

- A: 4 different cotton fabrics in shades of blackberry, each 5 x 5cm (2 x 2in)
- B: 4 different cotton fabrics in shades of blackberry, each 5 x 45cm (2 x 17¾in)
- C: cotton fabric in a blackberry pattern, 4 x 75cm (1½ x 29½in)
- D: cotton fabric in a blackberry pattern, 8 x 15cm (3¼ x 6in)
- F: cotton fabric in a blackberry pattern, 15 x 45cm (6 x 17¾in)
- G: thin iron-on volume fleece, 15 x 90cm (6 x 35½in)
- black hook and loop fastening, 2cm (¾in) wide, 8cm (3¼in)

Cutting out

Dimensions including 0.75cm (⅓in) seam allowance
- A: 4 squares a of 5 x 5cm (2 x 2in) (middle pieces)
- B: 4 strips b of 3.5 approx. 45cm (1½ x approx. 17¾in) (first border)
- C: 2 strips c of 2.5 x 33.5cm (1 x 13¼in) (strips for top/bottom edge)
- D: 2 rectangles d of 11.5 x 5cm (4½ x 2in) (sides)
- F: 1 rectangle f of 11.5 x 40.5cm (4½ x 16in) (back)
- G: 2 rectangles f of 11.5 x 40.5cm (4½ x 16in) (front/back)

Sewing

1 Sew 4 blocks as described for the small coaster, but consisting only of the middle piece and first border. Sew the blocks 'in a chain', as this will save time and thread. Only cut the threads between the piece at the end. Sew the blocks together at the sides with the right sides facing. Iron the seam allowances in one direction. Sew strips c to the top and bottom edges, and rectangles d to the sides. Iron the seam allowances towards the strips. Iron the fleece onto the wrong sides of the front and back. Place the two pieces together with the right sides facing and sew all around, leaving a turning opening. Trim the corners at an angle. Turn right side out and iron. Sink-stitch the blocks in matching thread.

2 Sew the hook side of the hook and loop fastening to the front of one rectangle d, and the fleecy side to the opposite side on the back.

Tip

Measure the circumference of your own pot. If it is wider, make the rectangles d wider to accommodate it.

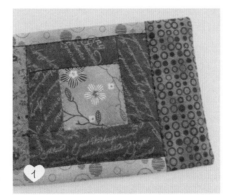

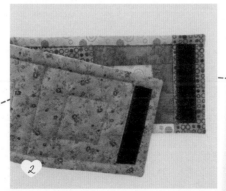

Materials

- A: cotton fabric with a motif, approx. 15 x 110cm (6 x 43¼in)
- B: cotton fabric with a motif, approx. 15 x 30cm (6 x 11¾in)
- C–G: 5 different cotton fabrics with motifs, each approx. 8 x 30cm (3¼ x 11¾in)
- H: black cotton fabric with a motif, 15 x 60cm (6 x 23½in)
- I: thin iron-on volume fleece, 25 x 35cm (9¾ x 13¾in)
- hook and loop fastening in a matching colour, 2cm (¾in) wide, 4cm (1½in) of each
- 1 spring snap hook for 20mm (¾in) tape

Cutting out

Dimensions and patterns including 0.75cm (⅓in) seam allowance.
- A: 1 strip a of 5 x 30cm (2 x 11¾in) (outside) 1 strip b of 8 x 110cm (3¼ x 43¼in) (tape) 1 rectangle c of 3 x 6cm (1¼ x 2½in) (loop)
- B: 1 strip a of 5 x 30cm (2 x 11¾in) (outside) 1 rectangle d of 5.5 x 21cm (2¼ x 8¼in) (flap outside)
- C–G: 1 strip a in each of 5 x 30cm (2 x 11¾in) (outside)
- H: 1 piece of pattern 3a (lining) 1 rectangle d of 5.5 x 21cm (2¼ x 8¼in) (flap lining)

Device Covers
Smartphone cover

Size: 13.5 x 9cm (5¼ x 3½in) (for a smartphone measuring approx. 11.5 x 6cm (4½ x 2½in) • **Level of difficulty:** ♡♡

How to do it

1 With the right sides facing, sew the long sides of the seven strips a together to make a large piece of fabric. (Note: If the smartphone is bigger than stated above, cut two strips a out of fabric A and sew eight strips a together.) Iron all the seam allowances in one direction.

2 Iron the fleece onto the back of the set of strips made from the strips a, and to the two rectangles d (flap) and the lining cut to pattern piece 3a. Cut pattern piece 3a out of paper. Place on the set of strips at a 45° angle and cut out.

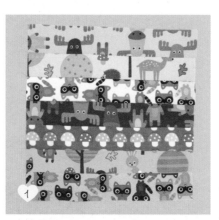

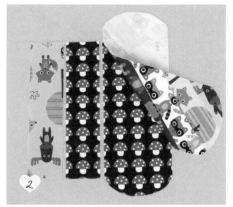

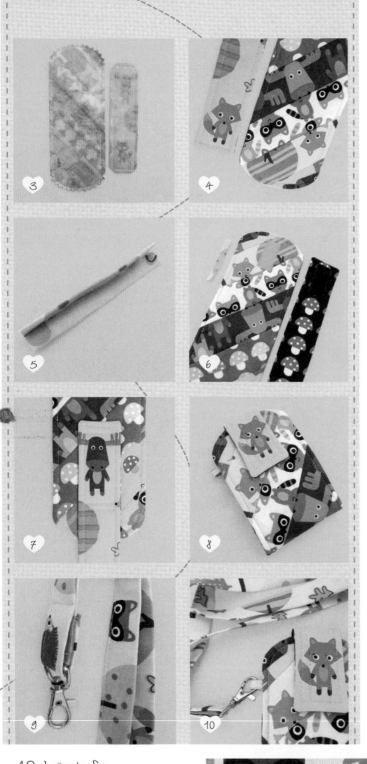

3 Place the pieces for the cover and rectangle d for the flap together with the right sides facing and sew all round, leaving a turning opening in the middle of one side. Snip tiny triangles out at the curves and cut the corners at an angle.

4 Turn the cover and flap right side out. Shape the curves and corners well and sew all around both items 0.5cm (¼in) from the edge.

5 To make the loop, fold rectangle c in half lengthways and iron. Open out, and fold the long sides towards the middle fold and iron, taking care not to iron out the middle fold. Fold the tape over so the folded sides are flush together. Iron, and edge stitch along the raw folded edges.

6 Position the two pieces of the hook and loop fastening in the middle of the outside of the cover and the inside of the flap respectively, and sew. The fleecy side of the tape should be 1cm (½in) from the top edge, the hook side of the tape 0.5cm (¼in).

7 Place the inside of the flap on the outside of the cover. The flap should protrude beyond the outside by 8cm (3¼in). Sew across the part of the flap that is on the outside four times, once on the existing flap seam and then again 5cm (2in), 7cm (2¾in) and 7.5cm (3in) from the first seam. Take care to sew only within the existing seam on the side of the flap, and secure at the beginnings and ends.

8 Fold the insides of the cover together. Fold the tape for the loop in half and push the ends into one side of the cover, leaving the loop protruding by 1.25cm (½in). Sew the long side of the cover together as far as the point where the curve begins, either by hand or on the machine, working along the existing seam on the cover so the loop is caught between the stitches.

9 For the tape, fold and sew strip b as described in step 5. Thread the tape through the D ring of the spring snap hook. Place the ends together so they overlap by about 2cm (¾in) and sew, then push the snap hook onto the end and sew the tape behind the overlap so the snap hook is attached to the end of the tape.

10 Attach the snap hook to the loop on the cover. A belt can be fitted through the sewn-on flap.

Materials

- ♥ A–B, D–G: 6 different cotton fabrics with motifs, each 10 x 110cm (4 x 43¼in)
- ♥ C: Cotton fabric with a motif, approx. 25 x 110cm (9¾ x 43¼in)
- ♥ H: black cotton fabric with a motif, 35 x 80cm (13¾ x 31½in)
- ♥ I: thin iron-on volume fleece, 60 x 80cm (23½ x 31½in)
- ♥ matching fleece tape, 2cm (¾in) wide, 8.5cm (3½in)
- ♥ matching hook and loop fastening, 2cm (¾in) wide, 2 pieces of 4.5cm (1¾in)

Cutting out

Dimensions and patterns including 0.75cm (⅓in) seam allowance.

- ♥ A–B: 2 strips a in each of 6 x 55cm (2½ x 21¾in) (outside)
- ♥ C: 2 strips a of 6 x 55cm (2½ x 21¾in) (outside) 1 of pattern piece 3b (flap outside)
- ♥ D–G: 2 strips a in each of 6 x 55cm (2½ x 21¾in) (outside)
- ♥ H: 1 rectangle b of 30 x 55cm (11¾ x 21¾in) (lining) 1 of pattern piece 3b (flap lining)
- ♥ I: 2 rectangles b of 30 x 55cm (11¾ x 21¾in) (outside, lining) 2 of pattern piece 3b (flap outside/lining)

Tablet cover

Size: 21.5 x 28.5cm (8½ x 11¼in) (for a tablet measuring approx. 19 x 24cm/7½ x 9½in) • **Level of difficulty:** ♡ ♡

How to do it

1 With the right sides facing, sew the long sides of the 14 strips a together in any order, offsetting each strip by 4.5cm (1¾in).

2 For the outside, cut a rectangle measuring 30 x 55cm (11¾ x 21¾in) out of the set of strips. The strips should be at a 45° angle from the sides of the rectangle. Iron fleece I onto the wrong side of the cut-out set of strips for the outside, to rectangle H/b for the lining, and onto the two cut-outs for the flaps in fabrics H and C. Then round off all four corners of the outside and lining using pattern piece 3c.

3 Place the outside and lining for the cover and flap together with the right sides facing and sew, leaving a turning opening in the middle of one of the side edges (cover) or along the straight top edge (flap). Trim the corner seam allowances and cut tiny triangles into the curves.

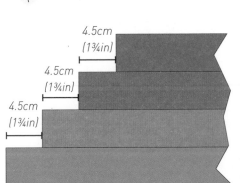

4.5cm (1¾in)
4.5cm (1¾in)
4.5cm (1¾in)

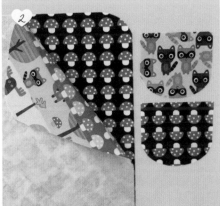

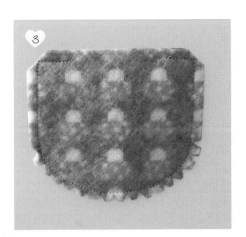

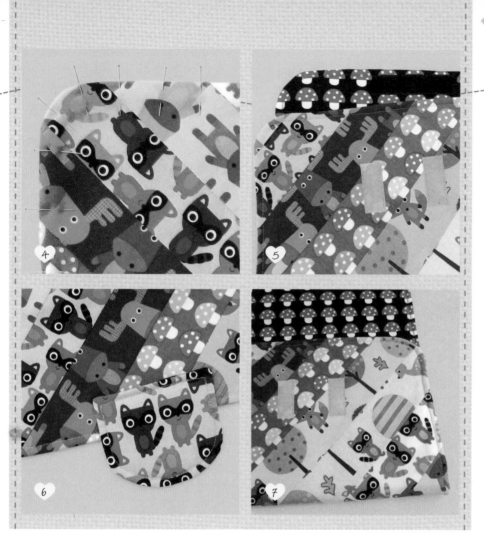

4 Turn the cover and flap right side out and shape the curves and corners well. Fold the seam allowances on the turning opening to the inside and sew them up by hand. Now sew all around both parts 0.5cm (¼in) from the edge in a slightly longer stitch (e.g. 3mm/⅛in).

5 Sew two pieces of hook and loop fastening to one end of the cover as shown in the photo. The strips will be 10cm (4in) from the side edges and 5.5cm (2¼in) from the top. Sew the fleecy side of the tape to the middle of the opposite end of the cover, 0.5cm (¼in) from the top edge.

6 Sew the flap onto the outside of the edge that has the fleecy side of the tape on the inside (this will cover the seams of the fleece tape). Position the flap in the middle of the edge and allow to overlap by 3cm (1¼in). Sew the flap only onto the existing seams on the cover.

7 Fold the bottom edge of the cover with the hook side of the tape up by about 19.5cm (7¾in) so the lining is together. Sew the side edges (either by hand or machine) together, 15cm (6in) from the existing seams on the cover.

Materials

- A–C, E–G: 6 different cotton fabrics with motifs, each 10 x 110cm (4 x 43¼in)
- D: cotton fabric with a motif, approx. 25 x 110cm (9¾ x 43¼in)
- H: black cotton fabric with a motif, 35 x 55cm (13¾ x 21¾in)
- I: thin iron-on volume fleece, 50 x 50cm (19¾ x 19¾in)
- matching fleece tape, 2cm (¾in) wide, 6cm (2½in)
- matching hook and loop fastening, 2cm (¾in) wide, 2 pieces of 4cm (1½in)

Cutting out

Dimensions and patterns including 0.75cm (⅓in) seam allowance

- A–C: 1 strip a each of 6 x 40cm (2½ x 15¾in) (outside)
- D: 2 strips a of 6 x 40cm (2½ x 15¾in) (outside) 1 of pattern piece 3d (flap outside)
- E–G: 2 strips a each of 6 x 40cm (2½ x 15¾in) (outside)
- H: 1 rectangle b of 18 x 49cm (7 x 19¼in) (lining) 1 of pattern piece 3d (flap lining)
- I: 2 rectangles b of 18 x 49cm (7 x 19¼in) (outside, lining) 2 of pattern piece 3d (flap outside/lining)

eBook reader cover

Size: 16 x 19cm (6¼ x 7½in) for an eBook measuring approx. 13 x 17cm/5 x 6¾in • **Level of difficulty:** ♡ ♡

How to do it

1 Sew the 11 strips a together as described for the tablet cover in step 1 (see page 51) and continue as per steps 2 to 4 (see page 52). For the outside, cut a rectangle measuring 18 x 49cm (7 x 19¼in) out of the set of strips, and again round off all the corners on the outside and lining using template 3c.

2 Sew two pieces of hook and loop fastening to one end of the cover as shown in the photo. The strips will be 5cm (2in) from the side edges and 4cm (1½in) from the top. Sew the fleecy side of the tape to the middle of the opposite end of the cover, 0.5cm (¼in) from the top edge.

3 Sew the flap onto the outside of the edge that has the fleece tape on the inside (this will cover the seams of the fleece tape). Position the flap in the middle of the edge, and allow to overlap by 2.5cm (1in). Sew the flap only onto the existing flap seams on the cover.

4 Fold up the bottom edge of the cover with the hook side of the tape by about 18cm (7in) so the lining is together. Sew the side edges (either by hand or machine) together, 14cm (5½in) from the existing seams on the cover.

Make-Up Bag

Materials

Details in height x width
- ♥ A: at least 5 different cotton fabrics in a light pattern, each approx. 15 x 40cm (6 x 15¾in)
- ♥ B: cotton fabric in a dark pattern, 45 x 50cm (17¾ x 19¾in)
- ♥ C: thick iron-on volume fleece, 35 x 25cm (13¾ x 9¾in)
- ♥ 50cm (19¾in) endless zip (1 half) and 1 zip pull, colour to match the edging
- ♥ sewing needle and thread (colour to match the edging)
- ♥ self-erasing marker pen

Cutting out

Dimensions including 0.75cm (⅓in) seam allowance
- ♥ A: 20 rectangles a of 9.5 x 7cm (3¾ x 2¾in) (outside)
- ♥ B: 1 strip b of 6.5 x 50cm (2¾ x 19¾in) (edging) 1 rectangle c of approx. 7.5 x 5cm (3 x 2in) (zip finish)
- ♥ lining cut out to fit the outside (see instructions)

Size: 17 x 23cm (6¾ x 9in) • **Template:** 4 on page 60 • **Level of difficulty:** ♡ ♡

How to do it

1 For the outside, arrange the 20 rectangles a in fabrics A in four rows of five rectangles. Sew the long sides of the rectangles together and iron the seam allowances of each row in the opposite direction to the last (see arrows). Then sew the areas together to make one single piece.

2 Iron the outside to fleece C and trim the overlaps. Machine sew through in the matching thread, either in soft wavy lines or as you like (quilt).

3 Fold the outside in half crosswise with the wrong sides facing and secure. Using the ruler and rotary cutter, trim the two side edges from the bottom (side edge) to the top at an angle to the first seam of the side edge. Using a marker pen, transfer the curved line to the top edge and cut freehand with the rotary cutter.

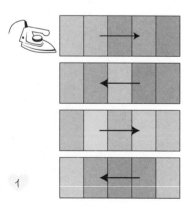

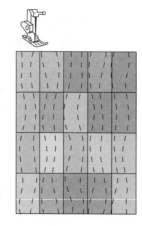

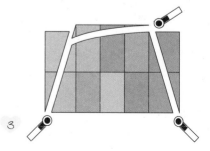

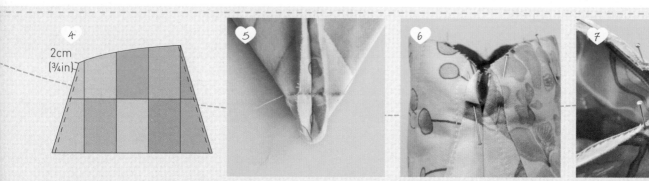

4 Open out the outside and place on the lining with the right sides facing, then cut the lining out to the same size. Fold the outside and the lining in half with the right sides facing. Sew the two side edges together (secure the beginning and end of the seam), stopping 2cm (¾in) short of the shorter edges.

5 Sew 3cm (1¼in) base corners in two corners of the outside and lining at 90° to the side seam. Put one side seam on the (planned) base seam to make a triangle, and sew. Trim the triangles back to the seam allowance from the seam.

6 Turn the outer bag right side out. Put the lining neatly into the outer bag with the wrong sides facing and the side seams together. Fold the seam allowances to the inside on the 2cm (¾in) side seam and sew up the seam below the zip between the outside and the lining by hand.

7 Fold edging strip b in half lengthwise with the wrong sides facing. Pin the raw edges around the outer bag, leaving at least 5cm (2in) protruding at the beginning and end. Unzip an endless zip; you will need only one half. Pin flush to the edge around the lining, folding a thin strip under. The teeth should be pointing down. The back of the zip will be on the lining. Leave 5cm (2in) protruding at the beginning and end.

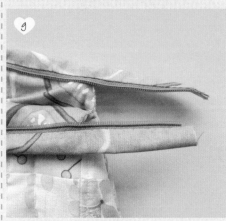

8 Use the zip foot (the needle is on the left) to sew along the zip teeth, catching all the layers in the seam.

9 Fold the edging strip to the inside and over the zip as far as the seam, and sew to the zip by hand using tiny hem stitches.

10 Thread the zip pull into the zip. Trim the edging and zip neatly, leaving about 4cm (1½in) protruding. Sew the short edges of rectangle c together with the right sides facing to make a tiny tube. Open out the seam allowances. Push the tube over the edging and zip with the right sides facing so the edges are flush together; the seam should be at the bottom. Sew up the open edges.

11 Pull the tube over the seam to the right. Push the cut edge slightly to the inside all round and sew up the opening by hand.

Tip

To make the zip easy to use, attach a zip pull to it,
or else make one out of little beads.

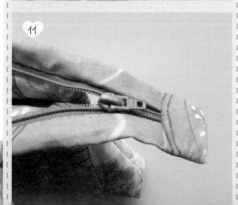

Wall Tidy

Size: 73 x 54cm (28¾ x 21¼in) (without loops) • Level of difficulty: ♡♡

Materials

- ♥ A: cotton fabric in a pink pattern, 55 x 110cm (21¾ x 43¼in)
- ♥ B: cotton fabric in a light blue and turquoise pattern, 30 x 65cm (11¾ x 25½in)
- ♥ C: cotton fabric in a light green pattern, 80 x 110cm (31½ x 43¼in)
- ♥ D: cotton fabric in plain pink, 45 x 110cm (17¾ x 43¼in)
- ♥ E: cotton fabric in plain orange, 10 x 70cm (4 x 27½in)
- ♥ F: cotton fabric in plain light green, 10 x 70cm (4 x 27½in)
- ♥ G: thick iron-on volume fleece, 60 x 80cm (23½ x 31½in)
- ♥ H: iron-on leather-like interfacing, 60 x 80cm (23½ x 31½in)

Cutting out

Dimensions including 0.75cm (⅓in) seam allowance

- ♥ A: 3 strips a of 8 x 110cm (3¼ x 43¼in) (border) 2 squares b of 14.5 x 14.5cm (5¾ x 5¾in) (back of pocket) 2 rectangles c of 26.5 x 14.5cm (10½ x 5¾in) (pocket)
- ♥ B: 2 squares b of 14.5 x 14.5cm (5¾ x 5¾in) (back of pocket) 2 rectangles c of 26.5 x 14.5cm (10½ x 5¾in) (pocket)
- ♥ C: 2 squares b of 14.5 x 14.5cm (5¾ x 5¾in) (back of pocket) 2 rectangles c of 26.5 x 14.5cm (10½ x 5¾in) (pocket) 1 rectangle d of 75 x 56cm (29½ x 22in) (back of wall tidy)
- ♥ D: 2 strips e 8 x 60cm (3¼ x 23½in) (edging right/left) 2 strips f of 8 x 53.5cm (3¼ x 21in) (edging top/bottom) 2 rectangles g of 8 x 14.5cm (3¼ x 5¾in) (first strip in block) 2 rectangles h of 8 x 21cm (3¼ x 8¼in) (second strip in block) 2 rectangles i of 8 x 19cm (3¼ x 7½in) (loops)
- ♥ E–F: 2 rectangles g each of 8 x 14.5cm (3¼ x 5¾in) (first strip in block) 2 rectangles h each of 8 x 21cm (3¼ x 8¼in) (second strip in block) 2 rectangles i each of 8 x 19cm (3¼ x 7½in) (loops)

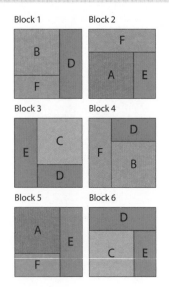

How to do it

1 For the pockets, fold all rectangles c together crosswise with the wrong sides facing (to 13.25 x 14.5cm/5¼ x 5¾in) and sew the folded edge at 1cm (½in) in the matching colour. Place the pockets on a pocket b in the same fabric and line up the bottom edge. Sew the first strip g to one side with the right sides facing (see diagram; the capital letters refer to the fabrics). Iron the seam allowance to the strip.

2 Sew the second strip h to one side with the right sides facing (see diagram). Again, iron the seam allowance to the strip. Continue like this to sew six blocks as per the diagram, then arrange in three rows of two blocks.

3 For the middle panel, sew two blocks together and iron the seam allowances away from the pocket towards one of the strips of the adjoining block. Then sew the rows together and iron all the seam allowances down. Sew strips e to the right and left of the middle section and iron the seam allowances to the outside. Sew strips f to the top and bottom of the middle section and again iron the seam allowances to the outside.

4 Iron fleece G to the wrong side of the front, and fleece H to the wrong side of rectangle d (the back of the wall tidy. Trim the overlaps. To make the loops, fold the six rectangles i in half lengthwise with the right sides facing, and sew up the long sides. Turn the strips right side out. Move the seam to the middle of the strip, then iron and fold in half (the seam should be on the inside).

5 Place the front neatly on the back with the wrong sides facing. Sink-stitch all the seams in the matching thread, starting with the seams in the blocks, then sew the rows and finally the edging. Trim the side of the back to the size of the front.

6 For the border, sew the short sides of the three strips a together with the right sides facing to make one long strip. Fold in half lengthways with the wrong sides facing, then pin the raw edges around the back part the wall tidy, starting at a side or the bottom edge of the wall tidy. Sew the loops evenly to the top of the wall tidy in any order (the outer loops should be about 3cm (1¼in) from the side edge). The ends should be at the top edge and the loops on the back. Leave about 20cm (7¾in) overlapping at the beginning and end of the border.

7 Fold the border up by 90° at one corner as shown in the photo.

8 Then fold the strip straight down again and pin. Continue until the case has been edged all round. Sew the border with 1cm (½in) seam allowances, finishing about 25cm (9¾in) from the beginning of the seam. Note: The strip for the border should be at least 10cm (4in) longer than required at the beginning and end.

9 Place the ends of the edge strip smoothly on the back and bring together in the middle. Insert a safety pin at the point where the fabrics meet.

10 Turn the border around the pin so they are at 90° to each other. Note: Do not remove or move the pin. Use a pen to draw a line through the insertion point of the pin (see broken line in photo) and sew the fabrics together along this line.

11 Check to make sure that the border is smooth. Trim the protruding ends to seam allowance width and sew the remaining section of the border.

12 Fold the border to the front all round and pin, laying the corners so that the folded edges are diagonal. Edge stitch the folded edges from the front. Fold the loops straight up on along the top so that they are included in the stitching.

Templates

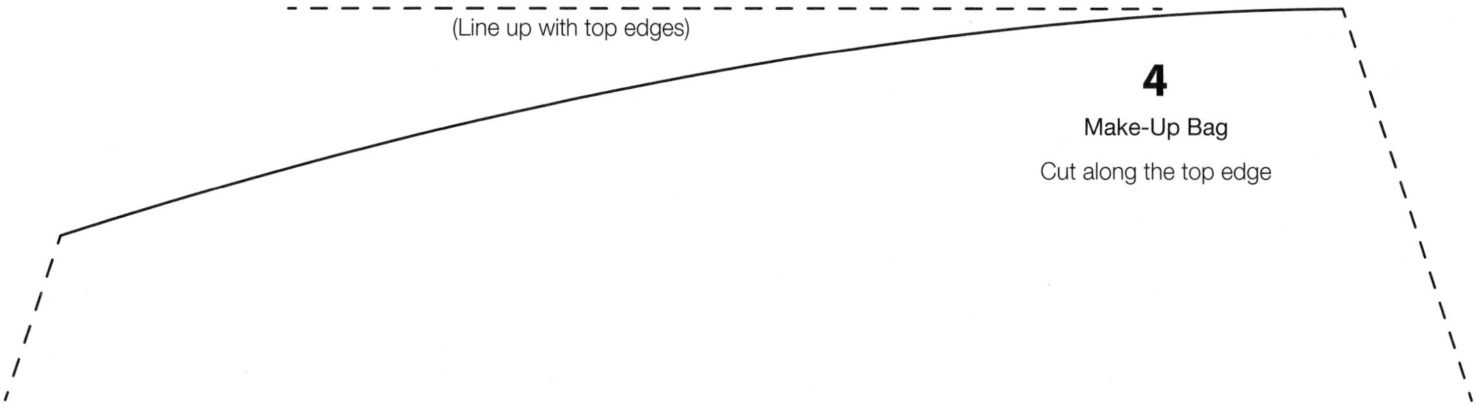

(Line up with top edges)

4

Make-Up Bag

Cut along the top edge

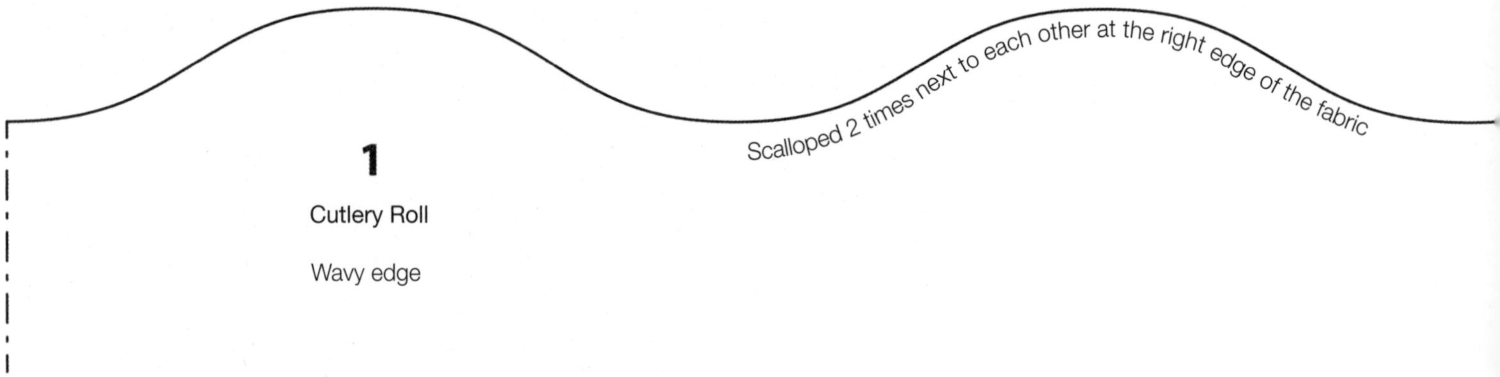

1

Cutlery Roll

Wavy edge

Scalloped 2 times next to each other at the right edge of the fabric

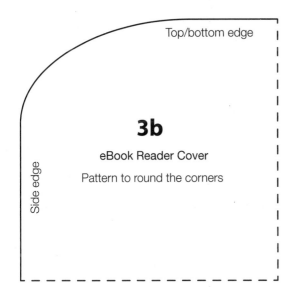

Top/bottom edge

Side edge

3b

eBook Reader Cover

Pattern to round the corners

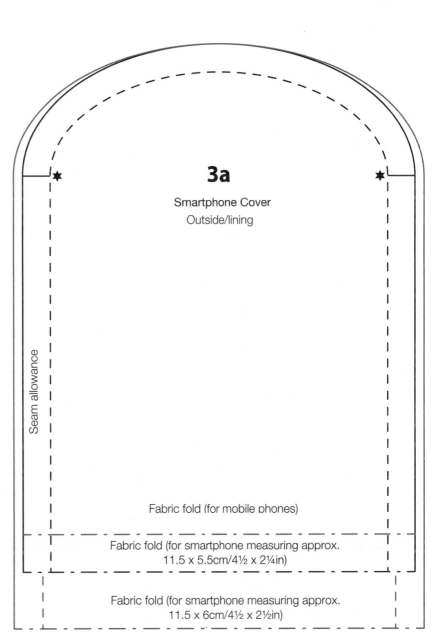

3a

Smartphone Cover

Outside/lining

Seam allowance

Fabric fold (for mobile phones)

Fabric fold (for smartphone measuring approx.
11.5 x 5.5cm/4½ x 2¼in)

Fabric fold (for smartphone measuring approx.
11.5 x 6cm/4½ x 2½in)

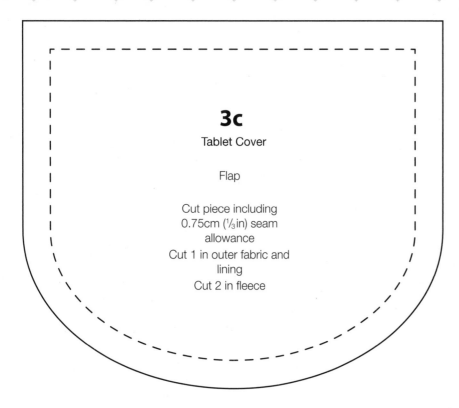

3c

Tablet Cover

Flap

Cut piece including
0.75cm (⅓in) seam
allowance
Cut 1 in outer fabric and
lining
Cut 2 in fleece

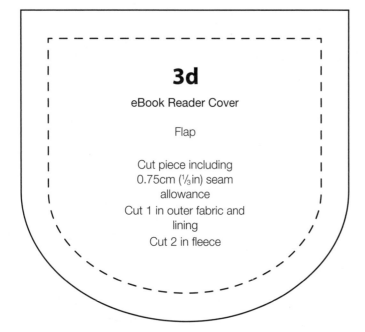

3d

eBook Reader Cover

Flap

Cut piece including
0.75cm (⅓in) seam
allowance
Cut 1 in outer fabric and
lining
Cut 2 in fleece

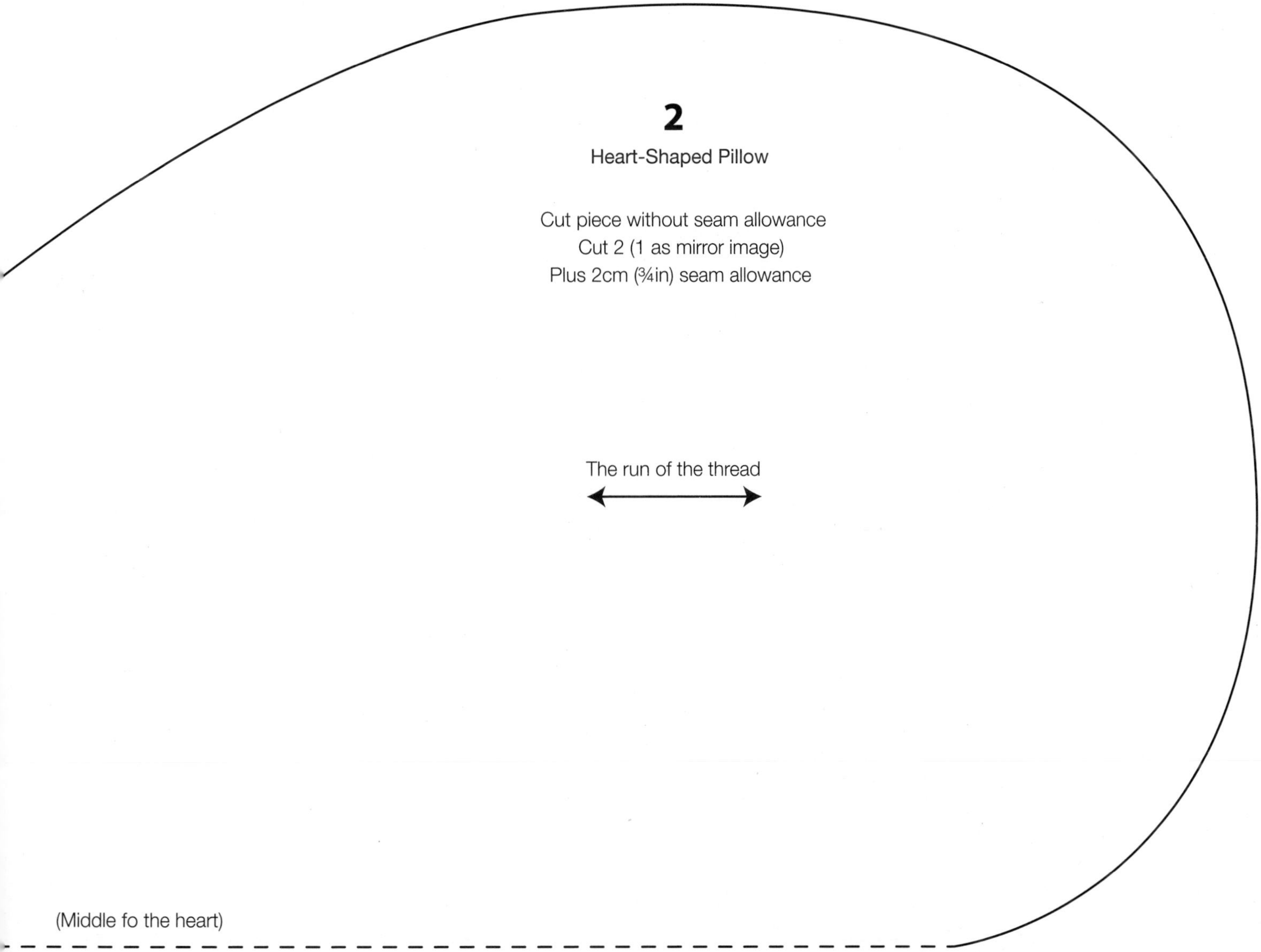

2

Heart-Shaped Pillow

Cut piece without seam allowance
Cut 2 (1 as mirror image)
Plus 2cm (¾in) seam allowance

The run of the thread
←——————→

(Middle fo the heart)